Lyddington Bede House

RUTLAND

CHARMIAN WOODFIELD BA, FSA, MIFA
and PAUL WOODFIELD RIBA, MIFA

Lyddington, a picturesque limestone village, lies on the northern edge of the valley of the River Welland, where a stream, the Hlyde, from which Lyddington takes its name, forms a tributary valley.

As the hunting to be had in the royal forest of Rockingham, on the southern bank of the Welland, appealed to the Norman kings, so the pleasures of the chase, with the proximity of royalty, influenced the Bishops of Lincoln to develop their estate at Lyddington, conveniently near the centre of the diocese to become an important seat of ecclesiastical administration.

This rural palace served the princes of the church up to the sequestration of episcopal property by the Crown in 1547. It passed to the Cecils of Burghley in 1600 and the buildings which survived were converted by Sir Thomas Cecil into the Jesus Hospital, later known as the Bede House, to house pensioners. It served this purpose for over 300 years, finally ceasing to be occupied about 1930. It was acquired by the Ministry of Works in 1954 and has since been restored and opened to the public.

ENGLISH HERITAGE · LONDON

CONTENTS

Unless otherwise stated illustrations are copyright English Heritage and the photographs were taken by the English Heritage Photographic Unit (Photo Library: 0207 973 3338)

Published by English Heritage
23 Savile Row, London W1S 2ET
© Copyright English Heritage 1988
First published by English Heritage 1988, reprinted 1993, 1996, 1999, 2001
Printed in England by ABC Printers
J78983, 08/01 C20 matrix 076368 FA7662
ISBN 1 85074 183 2

DESCRIPTION

South approach to the Bede House through the churchyard

Precinct wall and the gazebo

The first sight most visitors receive of the palace is Bishop Russell's elegant projecting octagonal lookout tower at the angle of the substantial high stone precinct walls. These were once backed by an earth bank to afford a high-level walk, with views from the first-storey octagonal room of the tower, outwards to the high road and inwards presumably to a Tudor garden; the windows are now blocked. There is a public passage at ground level through the tower. The bishop's arms can be seen in the centre of a quatrefoil panel facing over the road. [See the Glossary for a definition of technical terms.]

Archaeological observations made during drainage works behind the large precinct wall defining the western end of the churchyard showed the former presence of a very large ditch. The finds suggest it was becoming filled in the twelfth century. Further work has traced the ditch along the present High Street from the corner tower. The wall was later built along the line of the filled-in ditch. Aerial photographs suggest that the ditch turned at the north end and ran east, through the garden of the bungalow in Blue Coat Lane. This ditch, the earliest evidence of settlement on the site, is now interpreted as the enclosure of a late Saxon or early Norman manor, perhaps that of Waterius who is said to have held the manor in the time of William the Conqueror.

Surviving building

From the grassed area with the sycamore tree on the north side, the building appears as a long two-storeyed structure, near the centre of which is a gabled projection flanking the present entrance.

Archaeological evidence

The surviving building was not fully understood until drainage trenches cut in 1976 uncovered evidence showing that it is only the end cross wing of a great fourteenth-century hall, which ran from the face of the building as far as the gate to Blue Coat Lane. This hall was apparently built in the early fourteenth century, probably by Bishop Burghersh, and was 42ft (12.8m) wide internally, of four bays, some 76ft (23m) long, with a large two-bay buttressed porch at the northwest corner, and probably a similar porch at the eastern end of the cross passage.

Evidence for the removed eastern side wall of this hall can still be seen as a change in the masonry to the right of the three-light window. Internally the hall had a narrow walkway between the last bay containing the huge open hearth, where the sycamore tree stands, and led to the stair still standing in the gabled projecting structure. With the demolition of the hall the stair was retained to serve the Tudor almshouse.

Archaeology thus not only revealed the position and size of the hall, even greater than that being constructed by the Archbishop of Canterbury at Mayfield, Sussex, but something of its splendour: coloured tiled floor and green crested ridge tiles. More surprising was that below the floor there was an earlier narrower hall on the same alignment, the open hearths almost coinciding. The evidence for this pointed to a twelfth-century date.

To the north, beyond the enclosing wall, rescue excavations produced some evidence for a cross wing beyond the porches, similar in size to the surviving building. It would have contained the numerous stores for food and drink for the household and provisions for the visits of the bishop and his extensive retinue.

North front

With the two successive great halls established in this position, the surviving building can be interpreted as the withdrawing wing containing the finest rooms of the establishment. Inspection of the walling in the narrow passage between the stair tower and the main block shows squarish limestone quoins, diagonally cut with an axe, characteristic of Norman work. There is no other physical evidence for the early palace. If it does survive then all identifiable features have been lost in later reworking of the fabric.

At the right end of the main block a pathway passes through the building, dividing it from a tall narrower block to the west and aligned on a slightly different axis. Features on the north face, and within this structure, indicate that it was originally internal to a much larger block extending over the present adjacent garden. The greater extent of this block was also confirmed during rescue archaeological work in the 1970s.

Running along the front of the building is a lean-to veranda, erected in 1745 to provide some shelter for the old folk of the bede house. This rather obscures the canted projection of the wall where a lateral fireplace to the great chamber was inserted on the first floor. Two elaborately moulded doorways can be seen, surviving from the medieval building, one with crossed bowtell mouldings at the upper corners, a continental detail rare in Britain. The wall has been altered to accommodate fireplaces and windows to the bedesmen's rooms. In the corridor, hanging on the wall, is a fire hook for pulling thatch off the roof if a fire broke out. It was probably kept here to be readily accessible for any outbreak of fire in the village.

The Bede House from the north, showing the stair tower of the vanished fourteenth-century episcopal palace

To the east of the stair tower there is a chamfered medieval doorcase now leading to a further group of four bedesmen's rooms. This originally led to rooms in the eastward-projecting wing of the parlour range, probably an undercroft below the chapel, but the purpose of which cannot now be ascertained. Again archaeological evidence showed it to have been longer and wider.

South front

This handsome range, which makes a considerable impact from the churchyard, is largely the work of the late medieval building phase, augmented by post-medieval alterations.

Its most striking feature is the series of fine stone four-light windows at first-floor level, with a canted oriel window near the centre. The ground floor windows are by contrast utilitarian. The upper windows serve the great chamber and presence chamber of the bishop's apartments, with views over the churchyard to the south. To this front were added, early in the seventeenth century, two chimneystacks to serve the almshouse rooms. East of the oriel window the buttresses were rebuilt in 1767 when the two end bays were altered, but the third buttress from the right contains, at first-floor level, the garderobe for the great chamber.

To the west the passageway can be seen to be within the angled block, clearly of a different build from the main range. This appears to be originally a form of postern gatehouse, with a central doorway, the moulding indicating an early fourteenth-century date. This whole structure was apparently altered in the later building phase of 1480–1520 when the buttresses were added and the door was blocked off, to be replaced with the present passage. This was the result of a reorganisation of the internal plan, for a timber close-studded wall with a central arched door was built on to the new passageway.

Great chamber of the bishops, later the common hall of the Bede House

Ground floor

Bedesmen's rooms
On the ground floor, the medieval structure has been subdivided into a series of rooms by heavy oak-stud partitions, originally plastered. Each room has its own door, a fireplace and at least one small window. Furnished, these rooms would have provided handsome accommodation by the standards of the time and for most of the more than 300 years when they were occupied.

Excluding the present custodian's room, which was probably occupied by the warden, there are twelve rooms on the ground floor, presumably for all twelve men of the original ordinance, the two women probably occupying the two rooms formed out of the eastern end of the first floor. The structure was cut about severely to insert these fireplaces and their flues, and some ingenuity was employed to ensure that the window provided a view from

outside of the fireplace, no doubt a safety precaution to see the fire was doused at the close of day as much as to supervise the welfare of the occupant.

First floor

Stair to the ceremonial apartments
Ascending the stair, one comes to a landing area facing two fine doorcases, apparently dating from the early fourteenth century and probably surviving from the newly crenellated (fortified) residence of Bishop Burghersh. The shields in the spandrels may well have been painted and gilded but no trace of emblazonment now survives. On the right is a narrow chamfered doorcase which presumably led to a gallery above the vault.

Great chamber
The door on the right leads directly into the great chamber of the palace, a room no

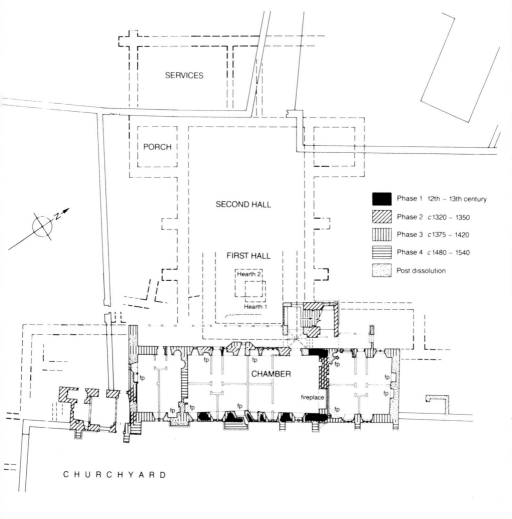

SERVICES

PORCH

SECOND HALL

FIRST HALL

Hearth 2

Hearth 1

Phase 1 12th – 13th century

Phase 2 c1320 – 1350

Phase 3 c1375 – 1420

Phase 4 c1480 – 1540

Post dissolution

CHAMBER

fp

fp

fp

fp

fp

fp

fp

fp

fp

fp

fireplace

CHURCHYARD

FIRST FLOOR

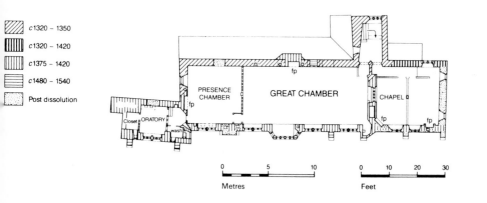

c1320 – 1350

c1320 – 1420

c1375 – 1420

c1480 – 1540

Post dissolution

PRESENCE CHAMBER

GREAT CHAMBER

CHAPEL

ORATORY

Closet

wash

fp

fp

fp

fp

0   5   10
Metres

0   10   20   30
Feet

Timber cornice to the ceiling of the great chamber

doubt originally sumptuously furnished in a manner appropriate to a prince of the church. The first sight of this chamber would have been awe inspiring to those who had been summoned to the bishop's presence. It is bathed in light from the handsome mullioned and transomed late fifteenth-century windows, with their rich contemporary, though reset, glass. Some bear the arms of various bishops of the see: St Hugh of Lincoln (azure, a saltire ermine between four fleurs de lys or); Bishop Bockingham (charge in the borders); Bishop Alnwick (argent, a cross moline sable); and Bishops Russell and Smith (argent, a chevron sable between three roses gules); their arms are similar and cannot be separately identified. Also to be found are the emblem and motto of Bishop Alnwick, DELECTARE IN DOMINO ('Delight in the Lord,' perhaps knowingly a hint of the Magnificat, Luke i 47), and Smith's motto

DOMINUS EXALTATIO MEA (perhaps another echo of the Magnificat 'The Lord has raised me up' i.e. from lowly estate). In the seventeenth century these mottos and martagon lilies still apparently filled these windows.

Below the exceptionally beautiful early sixteenth-century cornice, originally also richly coloured, the walls had fine tapestries and hangings, the close-set hooks for which survived until recently. The simplicity of the wall fireplace indicates the prominence given to the decoration. The bishop would have emerged from his inner chamber behind the timber wall at the end to greet visitors. To the right of the fireplace an inconspicuous door, now partly blocked, apparently gave access to the gallery overlooking the hall. Only the most privileged would have been invited beyond this point into the presence chamber itself, where no doubt, the more private discussions could take place between men of similar status, away from the ears of the officials and servants.

At the centre of the east wall there is an internal window of four cusped lights, within a recessed opening. Fixings for hinges show that it had shutters operated from the great chamber. The other side is set flush with the wall and finely moulded, indicating that the room beyond was of special status, probably the chapel. The mouldings suggest a date in the late fifteenth century. By means of this window the bishop and attendants would have been able to attend Mass without leaving the great chamber, the Mass generally being conducted by the bishop's personal chaplain.

Another convenience of the great chamber is the garderobe situated in the southeast corner of the room and ventilated through an opening in the external buttresses. It now has a sixteenth-century panelled door, similar to that forming a lobby to the main entrance.

Great chamber becomes the common hall

With the dispersal of the bishop's household it is probable that the fine furnishings were stripped out, anything of worth being sold to supplement the royal coffers. With the conversion to almshouses, this chamber became the common hall of the bedehouse, where the occupants were required to assemble three times a day for prayers and other communal activities.

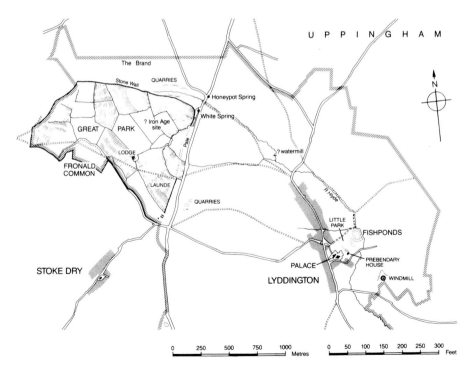

Parish of Lyddington with the Great and Little Parks, showing their relationship with the palace

Some fittings, such as the chest and the alms box are described in the foundation ordinances, a copy of which is on display in the custodian's room. The plain oak refectory table and benches, sufficient to seat the thirteen members of the household, and the lectern are probably also original furnishings.

The 'comon boxe' is set into the chapel window. Here visitors were asked to make their contribution to the hospital expenses, and it is where the occupants paid their fines for the various misdemeanours they might have committed, all carefully set out by Lord Burghley. These range from expulsion for heinous infringements of the rules, such as introducing and sleeping with one's wife, to the fine of one penny for peccadilloes such as 'blaspheming of God's Majesty.' Today their priorities appear rather curious.

Presence chamber

This room is identified as that in which the medieval bishops conducted their business. It has a fine fireplace with five carved panels datable by analogy to c1480–1520. There is also a blocked doorway originally leading up to the presumed gallery over the great hall. Here again there is some fine late medieval glass, notably the figure of a bishop and, above, the fragmentary remains of a prayer to the Virgin (possibly translated as 'O worthy Protectress who reigns in Heaven') and a small angel carrying a partial scroll with other evocations.

A door leads from this chamber to the attached building at the western end. The small lobby was clearly a space for personal ablutions, with a stone sink and draining place for toilet articles. Steps lead up to a small square well-lit chamber, perhaps a vestment wardrobe or private oratory. A large shaft in the northwest corner may indicate the former presence of a garderobe or flue. A blocked opening on the north wall, visible only from the exterior, suggests that communication may have existed with the parts of the structure now missing but known to have existed from archaeological work.

How the presence chamber was utilised by the hospital is not known. Communicating directly with the common hall, it is likely to have served as an administrative and records room, perhaps combined with the warden's lodging. There are no visible alterations of the post-medieval period.

Chamber at the east end

As noted previously, this space communicated by an internal window with the great chamber, contact being controllable only from that room. This suggests that the chapel lay here with the altar against the east wall.

Sixteenth-century rebuilding, followed by further works in the mid eighteenth century have removed any further evidence for the medieval arrangements. Now the room is subdivided to provide a corridor to the stairs to the attics and two further dwelling rooms for the almshouse, each fitted, as usual, with a fireplace and window.

Attic floor

In the medieval palace this space was probably no more than roof storage, perhaps where a house servant occasionally took his ease. Moulded tie beams, which can be seen where the floorboards have been removed, indicate that these were visible before the fine ceiling of the great chamber was inserted. Like the great chamber, part of the floor is laid in gypsum plaster on reed, a flooring technique common in the east Midlands from the late medieval period onwards.

At this level one can view the roof trusses at close hand, a series of fine knee-braced collar trusses with curved windbraces to

the single level of butt purlins. This highly
developed form of truss, shorn of
decorative frills, is generally found in late
medieval work, and again appears to be the
result of Bishops Russell and Smith's
building campaign.

The gabled dormer windows were
inserted in the seventeenth or possibly
eighteenth century. A small iron fireplace
indicates that at least one of the attic rooms
was used and heated in the nineteenth
century.

A step down at the far end leads to an
attic room in the western block.

The parks and fishponds

The Little Park

Leading away from the Bede House to the
north, the gated guardianship enclosure
gives way to a narrow lane called Blue
Coat Lane. The ancient name preserves
the memory of the garb to be worn by
bedesmen under the terms of Lord
Burghley's founding charter. This was a
blue cloak and black cap. At the north end
the lane opens out into Lyddington village
green, where the remains of the medieval
market-cross now stand. Immediately to
the right an unmetalled path leads to a
field gate and stile, and a path across the
field known as the Little Park to the
fishponds.

There are various references to the Little
Park in documents referring to the
Lyddington Palace. It seems to have been
the home garth of the palace, with small
pastures, orchards and, after c1320, the
fishponds.

The Fishponds

These survive now as major earthworks
sufficiently well preserved to enable one to
understand the main principles of their
use. The aim was to maintain and breed a
readily accessible and plentiful supply of

edible freshwater fish, usually bream, tench
and pike until carp were introduced in the
sixteenth-century, probably too late for the
palace.

The earthworks are rectangular and
consist of a deep perimeter moat with
external bank, the water being retained by
a dam at the southeast corner, now
breached. Within the moat, there is an
engineered system of three double troughs
which can be back flooded from the
perimeter moat at will by means of timber
sluices which do not, of course, survive
above ground. These troughs are further
interlinked by other leats providing
flexibility of management.

The scheme was devised to provide a
number of advantages. There was the deep
surrounding stock pond, or stew, which
additionally protected the interior from
unwanted marauders. Six interconnected
breeding tanks were made long and narrow
to give a maximum of shallow water edge,
which could be drained, restocked, or
netted whenever required. The spawn and
fry in the shallow margins could be
protected from predators by sinking
brushwood into the shallow waters. The
interior would provide a safe haven in
which water fowl could live and nest.

Although located at the bottom of the
Hlyde valley on waterlogged ground to
prevent drainage, the waters of the stream
were apparently not utilised, as sudden
floods from high ground could wash out
the breeding tanks and lose generations of
fish. Instead the stream was clearly diverted
around the eastern side of the perimeter
bank, and a more reliable supply of water
organised from within the Little Park itself:
run-off from the field and utilising the
small brook.

Probably added at some subsequent
period, an additional pond can be seen on
the upper side of the earthworks. This is
substantially deeper and well protected by
a bank. The only fish needing such

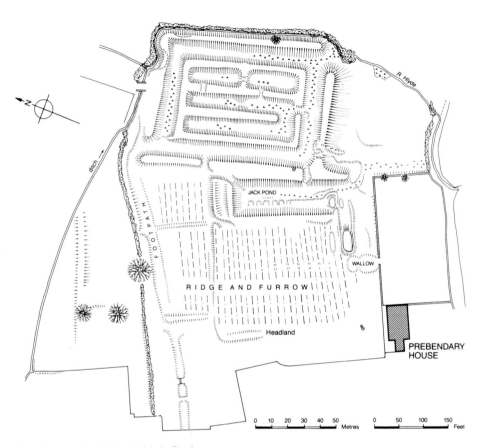

The Fishponds within the Little Park

separation and deeper water is the carnivorous jack or pike, a tasty game fish favoured from earliest times. This pond, set aside, is clearly the jack pond.

The fishponds are now usually dry. It has been claimed that they were built during the episcopacy of Bishop Henry Burghersh, 1320–40. They are undoubtedly a most important example of early hydraulic engineering on a major scale, demonstrating an understanding of fish management even earlier than the earliest extant treatise of William Taverner in the early sixteenth century.

Deerpark

The Great Park or Deerpark was built up through various grants of land through the thirteenth to the mid fourteenth centuries. It was a lightly wooded area enclosed by a pale or fence of tall cleft oak staves. The park was considered in rather the same light as the fishponds: a ready stock of fresh meat for the table available whenever required; but it had the added attraction of providing some 'sport' in hunting the captive animals, usually the red and fallow deer.

The medieval deerpark was thus understandably often not of very great extent, generally some 200–300 acres (80–120ha)—small compared with the great parks of the seventeenth- and eighteenth-century landowners. At Lyddington the location of the park recorded in documents was discovered only from a map of field names recorded in the Second World War by the composer, Stanford Robinson, working locally in the Home Guard. It is on the northwest boundary of the parish, on the high land, and can be traced on the ground in places as a modest bank and ditch—the ditch characteristically on the inside of the bank to prevent deer leaping out. Aerial photographs show a ditched enclosure within the park, probably from the Iron

Age, and much ridge and furrow dating from before its enclosure as a park.

Documents of 1227 record the grant of deer-leaps to the bishop. This honour, for such it was, entailed adjusting the earthwork to enable wild deer, the property of the King himself according to the law, to leap into the park without being able to jump out. Such features cannot now be identified with certainty. On the north side of the park, above the old stone pits, there are beneath the hedge the foundations of a stone boundary wall. It is possible that this is the stone enclosing wall for which permission was given in 1331, an expensive task that Bishop Burghersh may well never have completed. The maintenance of the pale was always a great financial burden.

The last reference to the deerpark was in 1602. It no longer exists on a map of the 1680s. Access to the Great Park appears to have been by one or more routes up the valley from the village, routes now preserved by footpaths. The best upstanding earthwork of the park pale can be seen from gaps in the hedgerow west of the A6003 above Lyddington. Modern agriculture has damaged much of the remaining circuit beyond easy recognition.

The church

Visitors to the Bede House should not miss the following points of interest.

The relationship of the church to the early moat has yet to be determined, for it seems the church was built anew in the fourteenth century on this site, possibly over the filled-in ditch.

The church owes its present form to two major building phases, that of the chancel being possibly undertaken by Bishop Burghersh in the early fourteenth century, with acoustic pots built in near the tops of the walls to improve the quality of the sound. This feature, the efficacy of which remains in doubt, is known in a

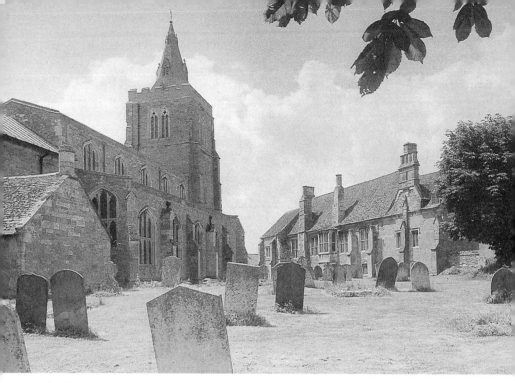

Southeast front of the Bede House from the churchyard

number of other places, large and small, and may be the result of high ecclesiastical patronage.

The nave is claimed to have been rebuilt by Bishop Alnwick and later bishops but architecturally the period of Alnwick's episcopate would seem most probable. Near its west end, facing the palace, is a blocked door, probably representing the private access of the bishop and his staff.

Fragments of medieval glass portraying a king and a bishop can be found in the tracery, and the church also has an interesting arrangement at the east end, where the post-Reformation communion table has been returned from the reformed central position to near the east end as advocated by Archbishop Laud (1573–1645). The protecting rails enclose the altar on all four sides, avoiding the creation of a separate sanctuary and allowing the laity access to the east end of the chancel, in line with earlier Puritan practice.

HISTORY

Early history

The date of the foundation of the medieval palace at Lyddington is not recorded. Archaeological research has shown that there existed on the site in the eleventh century a ditched and banked earthwork enclosing approximately 2½ acres (1ha). This was probably the manor held by Bardi, a Saxon thane, which was confiscated by William I and given to Remegius, the first Bishop of Lincoln.

The Domesday survey records that one Waterius 'holds of the Bishop of Lincoln, two hides at Lidentone.' Forty years later, in 1126, Pope Honorius issued a bull confirming the property as a possession of the church of Lincoln. There was a further affirmation by Pope Alexander III in 1163.

The fourth Norman Bishop, Robert de Chesney, received from King Henry II in 1154 a licence to till and have 20 acres (8ha) of land newly brought into cultivation at Lyddington. This suggests that soon after the civil war of Stephen's reign the bishops were seeking to extend their holding hereabout, and it must be presumed that they maintained at least a bailiff in the village.

On 25 January 1189/90 King John granted Bishop St Hugh of Avalon 100 acres (40ha) of 'ancient assart, quit of regard of the forest,' of which 25 acres (10ha) were at 'Lidinton in Roteland,' the remainder being at Lincoln and Spaldwick, Cambridgeshire. Hugh, who later witnessed Magna Carta, was succeeded in 1200 by Alexander. In 1209 his successor, Hugh of Wells, obtained a licence from the King to enclose, impark or assart his woods at Lyddington. This indicates that the succession of influential bishops had by then, if not earlier, seen Lyddington as more than a simple agricultural holding and were enjoying a good relationship with King John, a frequent visitor to his castle at Rockingham, almost within sight of Lyddington. This status is confirmed in 1209 by the promulgation by Bishop Hugh of Wells of orders for the repair of the bridge at Rockingham, crossing the Welland, addressed from his dwelling at Lyddington.

Clearly, by the first decade of the thirteenth century the bishops were not only staying with their extensive retinue at Lyddington, but were conducting business there—two activities which together can be taken to merit the seat being termed a bishop's palace. Up to this date the diocese of Lincoln had not only had a succession of distinguished and able bishops, but they had enthusiastically embraced the vigorous policy of building which had been adopted by the Norman church. It is therefore not improbable that the development of the rural holding to a palace took place earlier than the records quoted indicate, perhaps under the firm guidance of such men as Alexander the Magnificent (1123–43) or Robert de Chesney (1143–66), the builder of the palace at Lincoln itself.

After 1235 the great scholar-scientist known as the hammer of the monks (and of kings), Robert Grosseteste, visited Lyddington, instituting the first vicar in 1235, with frequent visits in 1237. He is better known for his authoritative reorganisation of the church than for building. A building is mentioned in 1226–63 when a certain Robert was hanged for stealing a ham from the bishop's pantry at Lyddington. Records continue with regular references to activity at Lyddington, perhaps one of the most

An impression of the palace buildings as they might have been in the medieval period (drawing by P Woodfield)

significant to history being the issuing from here of letters patent for the founding of Balliol College, Oxford, on 13 June 1284.

Fourteenth century

More is known of the history of Lyddington after 1320. The ambitious and unscrupulous young Bishop Henry Burghersh, who in 1330 baptised Edward the Black Prince, set about extending his hunting park. On 15 February 1329, when also Chancellor of England, he obtained Edward III's agreement to take in a further 20 acres (8ha), of assart and a few weeks later exclusive free warren in all demesne lands. A further licence was granted in 1331 to enlarge the park by 60 acres (24ha). By then the park had apparently arrived at its optimum size, for Burghersh obtained permission the same year to replace the park pale with a stone wall.

Burghersh's concern with buildings is marked first in 1329 when he obtained a licence to crenellate the palace at Lincoln. In 1334, with his appointment to the state Treasury to replace a murdered predecessor, the precariousness of high office perhaps motivated him to apply for further licences (which he received) to crenellate his palaces at Lyddington, and at Nettleham and Stow St Mary , both near Lincoln. It is unlikely that he had resolved to remodel on a grander scale all three palaces at once, so he was probably only regularising a position already *de facto* or at least well advanced. He is also said to have constructed the fishponds in the Little Park.

Burghersh, when in this country (for he is recorded as being frequently absent from the realm), usually resided within his diocese, enlarging among other activities his park at Tyngehurst (Fingest), Buckinghamshire, at the bitter expense of his neighbours, where he is said still to walk as its ghostly keeper. He is recorded frankly as being 'destitute of political morality.'

Burghersh was succeeded in 1340 by Thomas le Bek, and in 1347 by John Gynewell, who died while at Lyddington in 1363. His episcopacy was noted for his having to punish the University of Oxford for riotous conduct, and more distressingly, for the period of the Black Death which left Lyddington without a vicar for a period of time.

Fifteenth century

By the fifteenth century Lyddington had become a favoured house for the bishop and his retinue to stay in for some weeks from time to time. The registers of Bishops Richard Flemyng and William Grey show that they stayed regularly, conducting business and taking their ease, while Bishop William Alnwick, (1436–49) was another enthusiastic builder who again favoured Lyddington where possibly his portrait remains in the stained glass of the presence chamber. His great tower at the north end of the palace at Lincoln still bears his name, but, despite long-established belief that he rebuilt his palace here, no work demonstrably of his date can be identified with certainty. He may well have been enjoying the fruits of the work of his predecessors.

The last major phase of remodelling is attributed to two bishops: John Russell, (1480–94), chancellor under Richard III and described by Sir Thomas More as 'a wise mane and good, and of much experience, and one of the best learned men undoubtedly that England had in hys time,' and William Smith (1496–1514). From the evidence of the standing structure, it seems that their claim to have rebuilt the building is not far from the truth, for much of what can be seen today is the result of a building campaign extending from the later years of Russell's episcopacy, through that of Bishop Smith.

Internally, it seems, further alterations amounting to a refitting of the main audience chamber took place later, either in the last years of Bishop Smith's tenure, or subsequently, although it bears the arms of Russell or Smith. Ironically this splendid refit with its outstanding timber cornice, a peak of medieval interior decoration, seems to have happened only a decade or two before the final demise of the long line of illustrious occupants.

The end of the bishop's palace and the foundation of the almshouses

The house was surrendered to the commissioners on 26 August 1547 with much other episcopal property throughout the country. The property was passed by the Crown to Gregory Cromwell, then residing at Launde, reverting to William Cecil, Lord Burghley in 1600. Thomas, his son, founded a hospital called Jesus Hospital by deed dated the 6 November 1600, for twelve poor men, two women and a warden.

In March 1601 'Ordynaunces' for the government of the almshouses were made by Sir Thomas Cecil, Knight Baron of Burghley and Lord President of Her Majestey's Council of the North. They were to be locked up in the chest in the Common Hall, and they made provision for the clothing of the warden and brethren in 'gowneclothes of blewe' with black caps, and for them to be made a weekly allowance of 2 shillings and 4 pence, the warden 3 shillings, paid after evening prayers on Sunday, and an allowance of pit coal and wood for fuel. For these privileges they were expected to undertake not to be idle but to take on some handicraft while they

were able, and attend common prayer on Sunday, Wednesday, Friday and holidays, and all christenings and burials.

Selection of bedesmen was to be made by Lord Burghley himself, from candidates aged over thirty for men (forty-five for women), of good character with some honest trade or profession, free of leprosy, lunacy or the French pox. They were required to assemble for prayers at nine o'clock in the morning and again at nine at night before bed. Lord Burghley also devised a system of fines for non attendance, and for a range of other misdemeanours, the fines being put into the Common Box in the hall, which still survives.

The first warden was a gentleman, Paul Streatlye, and among the men were a tailor, a weaver, a shoemaker, Lord Burghley's groom, and a William Grumbolde, no doubt one of the well-known Northamptonshire family of masons.

The founding of the almshouse necessitated a major remodelling of the surviving structure. Unfortunately it is not known how much remained but no doubt there was some demolition and clearing, leaving the bishop's apartments to be subdivided to form simple living rooms for the fortunate few to benefit by Lord Burghley's charity.

In 1745 the present lean-to veranda was added to provide some shelter between the doors and the stair to the communal hall on the upper floor. In 1767 the northeast end was partially rebuilt, the end wall being set on a new alignment and further buttresses added to the churchyard elevation. Thus, with the proliferation of chimneys, the building took on its present appearance, continuing to serve as an almshouse until the twentieth century.

GLOSSARY

Assart   Piece of land taken into cultivation from the wild

Bedehouse   Dwelling of pensioners or bedesmen living under a rule laid down by the founder

Bowtell   In architecture, a small half-round moulding around openings

Bull   An edict of the Pope circulated to the dioceses under the holy seal

Buttress   Vertical projection from a wall to give additional strength or to resist the lateral thrust of an arch or roof

Canted oriel   Bay window with angled sides, on an upper floor

Close studding   Timber framing where the uprights or studs are placed close together, strictly no further apart than their own width

Crenellate   To fortify; in this sense to build or adapt a structure which could conceivably be used against the King and the law; a licence to crenellate implied royal trust

Cusped   With decorative rounded features or foils within an arch

Demesne   Estate, often the land close to or surrounding a manor or house

Dropped keystone   Decorative feature where the keystone (top stone) of an arch is emphasised by being extended below the inner edge of the arch

Emblazonment   In heraldry, the charges and devices on a coat of arms

Garderobe   Latrine, normally discharging into a cesspit or through an outer wall

Garth   Enclosure, yard or garden; area enclosed by cloister

Gazebo   Turret room with an extensive view, or a similar erection in a garden

Hide   Amount of land traditionally needed to support a family, usually 60–120 acres (25–50ha)

Leat   Open watercourse

Oriel   See *Canted oriel*

Pale   Enclosing fence, generally a stockade, and in deerparks with a bank and ditch

Postern   Secondary entrance, or gateway in a wall, often concealed and normally at the rear of a building

Precinct   Area of a monastery or similar establishment, enclosed by a substantial wall

Purlin   Longitudinal horizontal beam supporting the rafters of a roof

Quadripartite   Divided into four parts, in this context a vaulted ceiling divided by stone ribs

Quatrefoil   Four-lobed tracery

Quoin   Squared stone used to form the corner of a building

Spandrel   Triangular space above the haunch of an arch, within an enclosing moulding

Springing   Point from which an arch rises

Tracery   Decorative work formed by the branching of verticals (mullions) in the upper part of a window

Undercroft   Vaulted underground room of cellar supporting a principal chamber above

Warren   Area for keeping animals for hunting, especially rabbits; *Free warren*, the liberty to hunt